A WOMAN'S LIFE
ON THE EDGE OF
THE SEA

A Woman's Life on the Edge of the Sea

FOUR DECADES OF POETRY

Irene Skyriver

GREEN WRITERS PRESS | *Brattleboro, Vermont*

Printed in the United States

10 9 8 7 6 5 4 3 2 1

Green Writers Press is a Vermont-based publisher whose mission
is to spread a message of hope and renewal through the words and
images we publish. Throughout, we will adhere to our commitment to
preserving and protecting the natural resources of the earth. To that
end, a percentage of our proceeds will be donated to environmental
activist groups. Green Writers Press gratefully acknowledges support
from individual donors, friends, and readers to help support the
environment and our publishing initiative.

Giving Voice to Writers & Artists Who Will Make the World a Better Place
Green Writers Press | Brattleboro, Vermont
www.greenwriterspress.com

ISBN: 979-8-9870707-7-2

COVER PHOTO:
SUMMER MOON

PHOTO CREDIT FOR WATER/STRUGGLE
AND AIR/DEATH SECTION OPENERS: SUMMER MOON

PHOTO CREDIT FOR EARTH/BIRTH
AND FIRE/DESIRE SECTION OPENERS: GREGG BLOMBERG

Finnegan! We will meet you on the Other Side!

CONTENTS

IV: AIR/DEATH

I

WATER/STRUGGLE

From this wet womb
Has come
All Love   All War
And everything in between

Coyot

Coyot

Watchin' the river flow by
Watchin' the distant hills
Where once he roamed

Coyot
Long-braided man sitting
Long hours on river park bench
Kept by the fine company
Of other dark haired men
Who are not able to sit
And watch the river flow

As a matter of fact
They are out cold in the heat of the day
Sprawled haphazardly about

Coyot
Talk 'bout
"How's my spirit gonna go
From this park bench
Out over that river
Up into the sky
How's that gonna happen?"

Me: "Kinda like in the cartoons
You'll just start floatin' upwards
It'll be easy!

Coyot: "You know that"

Me: "But actually you might
Not go to heaven
You might go to hell
For gettin' in a fight with that black fella
The one you said kicked your front teeth"

We laugh

Coyot
He insults my big feet
And hairy legs

We laugh

Coyot
Of Chief Joseph's people
Nez Perce'
Watchin' the river flow by
And distant hills
Where once he roamed
Fierce bear hunter
Contemplating death
From a park bench
With bodies scattered about

-OMAK, 1987

Standoff at Standing Rock

Heading down the powwow highway
The Indian Nations are gathering
Their drums pound in resolute harmony
I ride a battered bus through the night
On worn-out seats I curl up fetal
Try to sleep

Eyes shut I toss and imagine
I'm in a trundling boxcar packed with others
On our way to smoking ovens
Or am I chained in the hold of a ship
Pitching in seawaters
I never would have dreamed to sail across.

The displaced
The dammed
Moved, traded, slaughtered like cattle

The American Indian too
Herded, corralled, culled
But their trail of tears may be evaporating
Transforming into thunderous clouds
And thundering drums

I follow their call to action
Knowing a great transformation
A rebirth of power and pride

Is blooming across a bruised and battered land
Through the voice of
A bruised and battered people
Indigenous wisdom re-found,
re-affirmed, re-formed
Here at Standing Rock
There in the Lummi Lands
And where the dams came down
On the Elwa River
Unification of First Nations

In the truly sacred struggle
To keep our waters wild and clean

I say A-HO! To them wherever they stand
Dance, sing or pray
I'm on my way to join
The only holy battle worth the fight
For our Earth Mother!

Sitting Bull

Like Sitting Bull in Buffalo Cody's Wild West Show
Like the Black man with his forced smile
Tapping his heart away
A tiger jumping through a ring of fire
A bear in a tutu—

I will not parade with my pagan lanterns
Singing songs of Earth reverence
For your holiday-shopper's amusement
I won't be dancing—

If ever our logic prevails
If ever the heartbeat of our Earth Mother
Becomes the highest concern of ALL humanity
Then our lights and songs will hold
A meaning, a revelation!

And by then
You won't be in an audience
You'll be with us
Singing and marching with a light of your own.

Me Too

"Me too movement"
Myself victim of rape
Forgave rapist
While in the act
Pitied him
For the wreck-of-a-human he was
As my innocent child slept peacefully
In the same bed

Margie 1999

Nuu-Chah-Nulth Princess
Almost 16
Northwest Coast beauty
Like a flower growing
On an impossible rock
The rock of white oppression
The stones of Christianity
The hard realities of substance abuse

From this you somehow grew
Bright and proud
Your ancestor's bones
Lie rotting in cold dark caves
And proud they too once were

If there is a glimmer
Of hope for your people now
It lies within you
Northwest Coast Princess
It lies in the twinkle of your eyes
And in the determination of your heart

Mexico 1979

Shanty shacks along the tracks
Black eyes
Buzzing flies

Unbelievable decibles blaring
At unbelievable early morning hours
From tinny speakers of tiny pueblo restaurants

"Christian brainwashed" women
Wade and wash fully clothed
In rivers bobbing with empty bleach bottles

Countless cases of empty Fanta pop containers
Stack one upon the other
Like spent ammunition
On the war against healthy teeth

The wonderfully warm ocean waters
Lick the littered beaches
as a dog would lick and clean a wound

Jungles screech sounds of a prehistoric era
As the young natives crawl into crowded beds
And dream of rock n' roll,
Hot dogs and apple pie

Arco Iris

Be like a rainbow of colors
Bound and bending together
Be not like the Red better off dead
Be not like an agent of Orange
And what of the Yellow Peril?
Forget about being Green with envy
Blues? Blues cannot be sustained
While witnessing Violet and Indigo
Band together
Bend together
As one brilliant rainbow
Let that rainbow include these colors:
Rusty Reds
Blueish Blacks
Burnished Browns
Golden Yellows
Creamy Whites
Let us all band and bend together

Crown of Light

We are all
Crowned royalty
When we stand under
The Rainbow of
Luminous lights
Even if we be
Bent and tortured
Through the prism
Of our hearts

Water is Life

Each day I take a drink
That comes from the hand-pump at my kitchen sink
I fill my cup 'til it hangs at the brim
I bend down close my eyes and sip it in
I imagine I'm at the shore of a wild river
Drinking in from this blessed Giver
Nary a drop goes down the drain
With climate change and little rain
This life blood of our Mother Earth
More valuable than gold in actual worth

II

FIRE/DESIRE

Like the Phoenix
Flying from fire renewed
Our hearts are lifted
To a new beginning

Lament of a single mother 1983

It is true
That to get the fruit
One can shake the tree

And shake it
I did
And fruitful
I have been

Yet I feel the branch
Breaking

Horses

Horses? Oh yes!
I've ridden them
Into saloons
Days into the mountains
Into the sea
Galloping nearly-naked down
Country roads
Racing them
Through Flower-festooned
Tibetan Highlands
Straddling their muscular bodies
As we buoyantly bob
In cool river-flows
Prance in 4th of July parades
Born again pagan
My red hand-prints
On their rumps

Open-to-the World

The night of
Thunder and Lightning
Sudden pandemonium
Waking me
In my bed open-to-the-world

Hair slanting across my face
Fingers gripping the blankets
Flashing neon Sky
Rain pelting my brow

So happy for this Magic show
So happy for the Rain
So happy for the down blankets
On this wintery January night
In my bed open-to-the-world
As Lightning stirs my tempered soul

Wren Amor

You walk through
this life
with intelligence
and grace
Always dreaming-up
something
with a smile on your face
You show us how
deep and high a mind can wander
while never
your sweet love
do you squander!

In the Arms of a Warrior 2021

A must-read
For apocalyptic times
This ancient tree
Gnarled fir
With a heroic hold
On cliffside thin of soil

Octopus arms
Stretched every which-way
Formidable roots reaching
Clinging tight

I
Swept into your arms
Like a warrior-saved child
Trying to fathom you
Understand your tortured stance
Might I survive this world
With as much beauty And dignity

Remembering in the face of
The grinding mega-machine
Your blood - you bled some on me
As you held me

That sweet smell
I do not wish to wash off

Are We Playing? 1986

Who's the king?
You wanna be on my team?
Are we bad guys?
Let's build a fort!
Stay off this rock!
Raise your hands!
Don't shoot!
I killed Raven already!
You have to say, "BANG!"
Is this your pistol?
You know when I'm aiming somewhere.
We'll set our knife right here.
Look at that gun over there.
Here's a knife!
I've got a high-powered rifle!
Yeah, but you gotta see my missile!
I can shoot anything out of it!
I have a pill to make me come back to life!
Oh yeah? What are you gonna do
if you're already dead?
You're on our team so guard our base!
Boom!
Missed me! Missed me!
And this is our crow's nest.
Musket. My musket!
My rifle!
Are we playing? Are we playing?

Maybe Fool's Gold

Waiting for the one in the still of the night
Waiting for the door to open quietly
For the tall and dark one in the dark of the night
To come through the door

Waiting for the soft voice in my ear
Waiting for the soft candlelight
To bathe his body in gold
Maybe fool's gold
All that glitters is not gold

Waiting for the touch
For the tangible truth
Waiting for love
Euphoric fantasy
Waiting Waiting Wanting

October Moon Puts the Hustle On

The moon rises from a veil of cloud
Like a dusky redhead who's just slept off the day
Ready to shake her voluptuous booty
All night long
Across the evening Sky
She has center stage
She will not share her bawdy act with stars
It is her night alone

She is not ashamed of her girth
Nor the pock-marked imperfections of her face
She is luminescent
She is in her glory
Shamelessly she chases the sun
Pursuing him for hours
Across her sky dance-floor

Whatever happens?
Does she finally win him over with her moves?
All we know is the Sun sure looks
Bright and happy
When HE rises in the morn!

Seven of Me

If only there were seven of me
One could be atop the orchard ladder
Yogi-like
Toes on the last rung clippers reaching
Contortion
Feeling the stretch
So many trees to go

Another me
Would be pulling weeds Rototiller-fingers flying along
Through soils cool and damp

Then there would be the me
To tidy the house
That's the me
I don't envy at all
Except when it's freezing

One me could happily be
Walking the goats up the mountain
Sipping wine as they find
Their forage
To make their sweet milk

Then of course
There'd be the me who'd
Milk goats in the wee hours

When the birds sing
And the one to tie the vineyard vines
And light the fire to cook the food
And lay with my lover

Wait! That's eight!
Besides I don't want anyone
Even if it's another me
Laying with my lover
That one I'll do myself

And which me
Would I let write?
Which could I trust
To dream my dreams
And sing my songs?

Fragmented by demands of spring
I long to do it all
But sadly
I am only one
Not seven

Two Spirit

Never was the "Brittney"
He stated out his being
To be
Rejection of frills
And ponytails
His trans – formation
Left behind
Skirts and lipstick
And gave me
My nephew Calvin
But
Before scalpels and implants
Indigenous Wisdom
Already understanding the reality of
Two Spirits
Accepting without carving and hormone therapy
A kinder inclusion of
Our trans-gender family

Fireman Son

What makes our young
Pick up a gun
March off to war
Strong in their core
Their duty to defend
To save
Those in peril
My son is such a one
His swords;
  A fire hose
  A ladder-truck
  His training to save lives
  His empathetic heart
Every day on duty
Not a soldier of fortune
For any passing conflict
But an everyday hero
Day after day
Year after year

Wolf and Otter

Twenty years later
On the thrilling outer shores
Of the wild and always unpredictable West Coast

Eagles seals seagulls
Whale otter salmon mackerel
Slanting rains
Ethereal deer
Burly bear
Warming in the sun
Gusting winds breaking waves

We were married
Like wolf and otter
Like wind and wave
Like fang and fur
We were meant to tussle and spar
Yet rise above with a
Steady love

Long after I am feeble
My mind will be alive
With the memory of
Your love
And this place

Willie

After the beautiful carnage of winter
There you ran
Fleet-footed
Barefooted
Mud squishing between your toes
Wild curls - matted hair
Crossing the greening fields
Heidi-esque in your beauty
And innocence
Even the goats raise their heads
In alarm
Who is this creature
Running
Calling out?
A child broke free
From the clutches
Of winter and covid times

Old Tree

You are the Old Tree
Moss covered
I sit against you
And feel your strength
Life force surging

You are the life force
I dish into
On our bed of dreams

Winds blow across our
Sleeping place
Mixing the ethers
Of our breaths

Our waking dreams too
Mingle as one
These many-seeming eons
"Playing House" together

Ah! Indeed
A hard man is
A good thing to find!

III

EARTH/BIRTH

To be born on the shores
Of this home so divine
Suckled on the breast
Of this succulent Earth
Spoon fed on sea breezes

Mother 2020

There is one Mother
She loves and
Feeds us all – our every meal
She gives us medicines
When we are ill
This Mother is not afraid
To show us Her ferocity
Or
On the turn of a heel
Caress us gently
She can be chaotic
And sick and
Scream with pain
For She is old
And headed for the grave
Yet She still moves
To show us Her wonders
The black velvet of Her depths
The glittering blue/greens of Her blood
Her foliage dresses and flowers crown
She does not want to die
In Her honor
I sing and laugh and cry

Winter Solstice

The trees
Dark and solid in silhouette
Stand as guardians
Huddled near and tight

From this bulwark
Reverberates the Grandparent Drum
Our Prayers
Songs
    Laughter
        Tears
Each bouncing before being caught
In the fire updraft
Shooting toward the heavens
Where those sounds are
Balm-like on a hurting

Above the tree crowns
The Cosmos slips by
In the time-lapse of our
Winter Solstice night
Heavy cloud
    Bright Moon
        Swirling Stars
Remind us of something beyond
This protection of our forest embrace

Cause and Effect

I step from the house
To the ground
And the lawn birds
Take flight

Causing
The small birds
At the feeder
To burst away

Causing
The wild ducks
On the pond
To swim towards each other

Causing
The Great Blue Heron
To unfold her vast wings
And leave the water's edge

Causing
The goats in the barn
To raise their
Horned heads

Causing
Me to begin my day
With a milk bucket
And a song

Born in the '50s

I was not born
So much as
Kidnapped from the
Womb of my mother

When doctors were god
"Let's just get things going!"
And no one questioned that
Especially a woman
Only there for a check-up
Prematurely
Horse-tranquillizer-induced
Strapped-down
Knocked-out

And there me
Tucked-up
Far away
Nowhere near ready for curtain call
Forced with forceps to take the stage
And brought home at 4.5 pounds

Babies Are My Gurus

There are *no* evil babies
Babies are my gurus
They are quickly corrupted
By over-adoration
By too much attention
Too little attention
Violence

They laugh they cry they poop
Uninhibited
They smile they accept they coo
They observe they trust
They understand humor
They are comforted by being held
Trusting in the arms of their tribe

Let me hold a baby
To remind me this
The true meaning
Of life and love

Owen

Coming strong and forceful
Like the storm into which he was born

He will be bright as a lightning strike
And as sweet as the falling rain

Cosmos Yariel Makah Cordova de Lopez

My baby's baby
Jumped off at "Earth Stop"
While riding the galactic star-ways
On a comet called Hale Bop

My baby's baby
Revealed himself from the vail of the womb
While a lunar eclipse
Vailed a full pregnant moon

My baby's baby
Emerged on the eve of the first fine spring day
After an equinox birth blessing
Where we all did sing and pray

My baby's baby
Entered this Earth-realm right
In the tranquility of the dark wood
On a frog singing night

My baby's baby
Was ushered in by the tone of a bell
A father, an uncle, a midwife
Three grand and two great-grand parents as well

My baby's baby
Is my new grandson
He's a beauty to behold
His soul, a cosmic one

Zoey

Along the slow and steady river
Your mother
Going with the flow and then
Back to the clinic
Surrendered to the steady rhythm
With the grace of a dancer
Doing *The Dance*

Unexpectedly
Soft energies screech to a halt
As a grandmother's concerns
From miles away   reach
"You know she had an aneurism once"
Birth clinic says it's a game changer
The birth must happen at the hospital

Anger and determination
Now the focus
"I'll give birth on your lawn
before I go to any hospital!"

Courage and Janis-like fortitude
And out came Zoey
Before any attempt could be made
Toward an institutional birth

Baby girl born of strong will
Happy birthday!

Rio Elan Makah Cordova de Lopez

The first rains of autumn fell
And created a river
A river that could not
Would not
Refused to be held back

It coursed with a briskness
Of energy that was powerfully humbling
It tumbled on its way with sparkling effervescence

Your mother
Your father
Your brother
Your grandfather
Your uncle
Your neighbors

Your auntie
And your grandmother

Oh with what spirit
You splashed upon me - you lively river

We stood by the shores of your mother's womb
We awaited you with trembling excitement
Indeed you were like a flash flood
Into our hearts
When with vigor you burst the dam

And I scooped you up
Like the sacred river water that you are
And I was reborn by the magic of you
Gracias Rio Elan!

Aviva

It was a star-filled flight
To your place of birth
Mother and father didn't
Have it planned that way
You have your own ideas
Flying from the island

Taken to a room where
Men do miraculous
Things with scalpels

I listened for your cry
From just around the corner
I followed you "little unknown"
So that I could know you

I said "please let me hold her"
Back and forth in the glass room
I walked with you
You hollering "what the heck is this all about?"

After certain realities
Had been surrendered to
By us all
Daddy and I ran
Clenched fists raised
Shouting down the street
"AVIVA LA REVELUTION!!!"

Leaping Waters Girl

Talula came
When her uncle died
Enter stage right
Exit stage left

Brother leaving brother
Bad-news-phone Drops
to the floor

Leaping-Waters-Girl
Laying alone
Vulnerable

Easy come life
Easy go life

Let me protect you small one
Tears of emotion

New baby grows within *me*
Easy come life
Easy cum
Easy
Go

Oliver

Our grandson
Bright as sunlight on a glacier
Bouncing the light back
A flashing mirror of all you see
An astute study of character
A born entertainer
Gifting laughter and rapture
Bright brave soul
Walking forward with a bounce
To your step
As you hold the spirit-hand
Of your older brother

The Crack

The slit in the cliff
Earth yoni
Into which I determined to
Squeeeeze myself
My son – my doula assists
"rest"
Careful descent
Inching squeezing
Remember my breathing
Finger-width toe holds
Cool cleft pressing
Being born back into the Earth
Encouragement from my son/doula
"breathe, you're almost there"
Finally an opening
I'm in the cave
With a view out
From the mighty sheer cliff
Marine-green depths of water
Far
Below
This sanctuary in the womb
Of our Mother
A temple of her own making
We burn copal
And give thanks
My doula and I
In no hurry to
Undertake
Our reverse birth

Juniper

An anomaly among modern youth
Keeper of traditions
Decades of gifts stealthily left on our doorstep:
Mayday flowers
Solstice gift baskets brimming with sweets and nuts
Needlepoint embroidery
Countless cards hand-painted dreamy and bucolic

A recorder of family history
Listener
Ready farm helper
all heart
She is her own grandma
Our only grand-daughter
A short path away

Ringing in the New Year

Almost like an Ecstasy-laced love fest
We trance-danced our way into 2023
The hall was full
The horns, guitars, drums
And the singer's voices -
Like a call to prayer from a minaret
Carrying our frenzied bodies and smiles

We were caught in a web
Of a huge inter-connected fishing net
It held us and brought closer and closer
As we were drawn upwards higher and higher
From the three-year COVID bottom
All to the same level of ecstatic bliss
A re-bonding of hearts and joy
Even if by the next day we be put on ice and sold
To the next gluttonous pandemic
It was not a fisherman's tale
Our love of each other last night

Raven Glass Artist

Born into a tribe
Of onlookers
Handed around each to hold
Looking into the eyes of community
Growing strong in the knowing
Of love and support

Fed on the beauty of nature
Internalizing shapes and colors
Nourishment for his future work

The Sockeye salmon flashing
Through emerald waters
Watery eyes of curious seals
Popping up near the shores
Spouting whales
Slinking otter

Future subjects of sculpture
Wrought from molten glass
Fearless   in fact joyful
In his dance of perfection
A Joy to behold
My son Raven

Few Saints are Born

More likely
We are ALL born saints
But we forget that LIGHT
Intrinsic
We learn greed and self-preservation
Not so my daughter
Pure of heart and tireless giving
Endless durability of body and heart
Giving of:
Time-work-money-flowers-food-compassion-laughter-
dance-touch
Add any additional saintly qualities
And she is surely those as well
Did she come
In part from ME?
How can that be?
My daughter Summer Moon

The Indigenous and Damn Hippies Were Right!

Make **Love** not war – **Yes!**
Eat **Organic – Of course!**
Live **Simply – Why Not?**
This morning's news: **Psychedelics** Legalized
For their benefits on the mind – **Duh!**
Grow Your Own – **You are** what you eat!
Two-Spirit – Our **Bi-Family!**
Bare feet on the **Earth – Good Feeling!**
Mud Houses/Tipi's – **Coool!**
Circle Songs of Reverence – **Sing Out!**
Flower Power – **Trippy!**
The Earth is our **Mother – Earth Children!**
Sky Father – Sacred air that we **breathe!**
First Nations Peoples and **Hippies – True Wisdom,**
  not a passing fad!

IV

AIR/DEATH

Oh trickster Raven
What have you up your sleeve?
What stories of Ancient ones?

Make us laugh
We care not to grieve

My Mother Mary 2002

IYEE! A deep cry from the
Pit of my being
Oh mother dear one
So now you've done it
The unthinkable

You've left me an orphan
Wailing miserably into
The winter gale

You, such a monument to simplicity
Only love mattered
You, who I could never imagine not having
Yet know physical "having"
To be so shallow

You, who owned nothing but the slick red car
And even that was not "about the car"
It was your time machine
Magically delivering you
Through time and space
To each of your scattered offspring

Each of us with our own unique plans of how
To spend our short time with you
And then you were off in the red car
An emissary on missions of mothering

Then came news of your illness
An alien invader
It moved in on you
FAST!

As you laid there oh-so-tiny
Withered to skin and bone

I rested my head on your sharp shoulder
And was compelled to whisper
"I wish I could be your baby again"

I did not expect your skeletal arm to move
It inched from your nearly spent body
And patted my back
Gently Motherly
Like burping a baby

The depth of what I was on the brink of losing
Flooded
I would be nobody's baby anymore
Her patting
Her final loving gesture
My last chance to be her baby

Back on my bluff
As I cry baby-like snot and drool
Into an irritating wind

As if to remind me
Of the comfort I may no longer
Seek in your arms
Your smile
Your humor

There seems no justice in this

I don't want just memories of you
I want YOU!
You, a monument to simplicity
Only love mattered
Only love mattered

Father Don Petroleum Barrett II

He dreamed
He was a dreamer
Even as a child in the orphanage
Where he protected his brother
And idolized Charles Lindbergh
And Imagined flying free someday

The brothers farmed-out as child labor
The Great Depression — hard times
But he dreamed
He dreamed of flying
Far above the dirt and toil of the fields
His head was   up there

Married the dirt-poor farmer's daughter
Survived World War II
I am their fifth child my brother their sixth
Still dirt poor but working angles
Becomes caretaker of a small airfield
Now! Now he could take to the heavens
Dipping diving barrel-rolling FREE!

Off to Alaska he flew
Would he find his native father?
Off to Alaskan oil-fields he flew

His two-seater plane
Flying low along the West Coast
Summers without Dad

Returning with tanned moccasins for me
And stories
Wrestling tickling tumbling play time again
It was a Man's World
But I had the advantages of a tomboy

Age 69 given cancer death-sentence
One year
He used it to learn accordion
And surprised me with his parting song
Irene Goodnight
And too
Surprised the hospital staff
"I guess you're wondering why
I've asked you all here"
Humor for the staff
Who were to give him his lethal dose
And his final flight to the heavens

For Sally

I've thought of family
As being a river
We each step into
From different shores of time
But I reevaluate now
The day of my sisters passing

Now I think it more
A torrent
Our family
Swept along
Each in turn from birth
Until branching to create
Our own stream

In the short time as we
Six kids bobbed
Or were swept along
In simmering
Roiling
Sometimes violent waters
Occasionally
The water would level
And we'd find ourselves
In a splendid pool
Laughing and playing
Together

A river is a natural
Living thing
Most dangerous when
Dammed

Our family was swept along
By effects of broken dams
Damages of

The Great Depression
WWII
Inequalities of the sexes
Poor food
Abandonment

These were boulders dodged
In our river
Until we gingerly stepped out
Dried ourselves off
And went to find our own path
Our own waterway

We did not look back much
We loved our parent river
And forgave for the sometimes-rough ride
We even wished mightily

That we COULD step back
Into that imperfect flow
So we straggled
Not too far

For our love of that river
Runs deep

Now we reflect
On the deep pools
The glittering reflections
The humor and goodness
The place of our connected hearts

Time has brought us to
A wide valley
Made fertile by
The grinding of rock and wood
It is in this green vibrant expanse
That I see
Honor and love
My sister Sally

Particles of Dust

Particles of Dust - written in boyish script
Across the head of your trap-set base
Your first band
Beatles   Rolling Stones   Jimi Hendrix
Even your own tunes

From where did your musical talents bubble up?
Youngest of six
Me right before
You
Not a one of us with your gifts

I have always had rhythm
And love to sing
Maybe you're the reason I sing
And dance

Earlier
The two of us   little scoundrels
Trouble makers
Explorers   tree climbers
Inseparable

Now separated
You slip away from a brain that
Turned to jell your intelligence
Me left to rub away the dust
To remember the true you
My brother

Community Brothers

For the brother
That laughed
The sky cries
For the brother who drummed
Thunder booms
For the brother who juggled
Stars shoot
For the brother who embraced
Sunlight warms

As if
The earth opened
And swallowed our beloveds
Yet we will remember them

In the clear rain
In the clap of thunder
In the shooting star
In the comfort of the sun

Doomsday Clock

Myself conceived
At the time of the first hydrogen bomb
Detonation

The Doomsday Clock started
When I started my wombs-day clock
We're both still ticking in 2021
There are only 100 seconds left
Or - 7 years, 103 days, 15 hours and 40 minutes
Myself and my Earth
At the midnight of our time

We cannot undo what men have done
Before we were even born
All we can do is sing to the twinkling stars
Love the lofty thunder clouds
Tickle babies' feet
Grow our own food
Tell ridiculous jokes
And make love not war

Go slow
Time is running out!

A Morning Mourning the Salish Sea

The clouds
Like racks of fish bones
And fading contrails share
A bleached-blue sky
That hangs above
A still, desolate sea

No fin, fur or feather
Break the surface
For miles in all directions
The Salish Sea lies
Flat and undisturbed
In the most disturbing way

Where is the whale
Or flocks of gull
Where is the sleek seal
Salmon school
The flash of herring

Where is the Sea Star
The kelp tangles
The blue muscle-encrusted capes

Like a wanderer in desert sands
I am parched by the bleak
Emptiness of the sea

Malena

Millions of
snowflakes falling
On this day you left

Millions falling
Softly
Silently
Each to magically vanish
As it touches
Down on Earth

Each beautiful
Each soft
Each perfect
Falling Falling

Kayaking Amid Spirits 1995

There's a haunting quiet
A vicious void
Totems decayed
Skulls growing moss

There's a scoured seascape
No canoe or paddler in sight
Rotting remains of tooled wood
Laying in dark caves of the dead

Breezes breathing soul-filled sighs
As they push at my back
Urging me onward
Into the watery routes
Of a time lost

West Coast Burial Island

Where but for those shimmering beaches
Walking in the footprints
Of Cougar, Bear and Wolf

You opened the book
To my own past
Calling back in breathy voices
From burial canoes

Canoes now flocked
In depths of iridescent moss
And there, clearly
A scull
And another and another
Passengers yet
On their Journey Of The Dead

Looking out through mossy eye sockets
Vessels that now resemble more the forest floor
Sinking into it
Like the ocean itself

You took me behind the green veil
Beyond the fringe that obscured a past
Magician's slight of hand

Old Man Time
Whose shape-shifting trickery

Takes place at glacial speed
And yet the changes
Have happened In a blur
In a blink

Children once laughed here
Totems told their stories
Now almost silenced
Their carved lineages lay
Like the burial canoes
Face down, muffled in the duff
Of pine and fir and cedar
Their breaks and maws muted
By rot and smothering moss

Perhaps the greatest gift given,
This insight
Reaching back
Through decay and skeletal remains

To the days of hope, joy and longing
Of power and pride
That bring a new humbleness
While treading on sands wiped clean of
All that past
But that which Cougar, Bear and Wolf
Have never forgotten

For Roy Prestholt 1982

Today I saw the remains of a man
Wheeled from surgery
A feeble, skeletal, gray-stubble form
Crying out in pain

Instinctively we clenched our hands together
He, wanting the fresh charge of life
Sent coursing from me to him
I, wanting to provide it

So much of a bright man
Loving man
Now reduced
One lung less
Looking small

Oh what does it matter to the Universe
That he was a bachelor all his life
That he ran for the joy of it
That he baked sweets and breads
That he wore bright shirts and liked soap operas

What does it matter to the Universe
That I love you Roy
I think it matters
I know it matters

Melvin Marlin Scriver, 1954–2022

Our love was real at 17
Our love was real when we conceived our girl
Our love was real when we conceived our boy
Your kind heart and humor were real

Mel and Son Electric – complete with ritual
after-work drinking
Flying sewing machines and dishes
Fist holes in walls
Those were real too

Fear of a life spent this way
Fight or flight?
I chose flight
But never un-loved you

A fear-filled unknown
My journey with babies
As your path took you
Still deeper
The chasm of our hearts widened
But I never un-loved you

Our children conceived of love
Pulled you back
From the long dark journey
Into our lives

Your enduring kind heart
Humor and ingenuity

Blessing us and all
Who came to know you

Mother of your children
Thankful for the second chance
To know why I loved you
None too soon

Now you have joined the growing legions
Of loved-ones Crossed-Over
Into the illuminating sprits
Of meteors, stars and sun
Hear me
I never un-loved you

For my grandson - Finnegan Marlin Scriver
1/30/2003 – 8/1/2021

His oil and dirt permeated shirt
Tells only one attribute of my grandson
I hold it to my face and breathe it in
As if it were perfume
The fragrances of his mechanical skills
His shovel-ready willingness
His muscle strength and grace

But he was more than a boy/man
Unafraid of work
He was a god
I kid you not!

He could leap through the air
And fly in a single bound!
But his soul was grounded
In tenderness and love

He did not shy away from joy
Any more than he did from work
A boy/god/man so supremely physical

He had to feel speed and music pounding
But could also slow down
To love a baby or smell a flower
Or be a team player of heart and skill

Light and beauty beamed
From his eyes and smiles

Of the purest essence
All this in ONE young man

So bursting with life
It could not be contained
He streaked through our lives
Like a falling star
Fast and spectacular
A god
I kid you not!

Chadwick Bluff for Finnegan

From this glistening
Snow-topped promontory
A lone Golden Eagle glides
At cliff's edge
Catching the up-draft
And I too am lifted
Lifted by the effortless flight
And dazzled by the riches
Of snow diamonds
Scattered at my feet

I remember your spirit
Alive and dazzling on this same precipice
Your spirit – infectious and contagious
Up-lifting and sparkling
Eyes as bright and blinding as the snow
I will remember you too
on this high and daring cliff
As a spirit ever-soaring
And golden

Marcelo's Lounge

What a life!
Where did their spirits and pride go?
Is the white man such a terrible leach
That all red mans life past and present
Is sucked from them never to return?

How powerful an evil must be
To crush a people so totally
Their life seems as gone
As the last drops of beer
That dribble from the can to the floor
As the clutch of the hand relaxes

Their proud spirits are as vanished
As the "Indian Money"
From their tattered wallets
Gone is the gleam in the eyes
Decayed are the teeth in the mouths
Short the blue-black hair
Long are the hours spent at Marcelo's Lounge

- JUNEAU ALASKA, 1976

Pushing Seventy and Counting the Miles

Like a Tibetan prostrating
thousands of bendings
but - to the garden soils
blessing the seeds pulling the weeds
Reaping the gifts of harvest

Miles danced across floors and around fires
Multitudes of minutes in orgasm
A life lived ecstatically
Conceiving from fathoms and heights

To recoil from loss
and curse the blind
The ignorance in the world
the deaf
the wicked
the barbaric

Embrace me dear lover
Dear family
Horrible enemy
I'm not long for the world
I would like to dance on your grave
But you may dance on mine
And that is fine

Don't Let Me Go 2017

I want to die in your arms
You who have always comforted me
Let me curl up
On your cold stone
'Till I turn to bone

Let me sink to the depths
Of your salty seas
Let me stand on your glaciers
Until I freeze

Let me dry to dust
In your desert sands
Just don't let me go
At the hand of man

Contemplating Sky Burial

Promises to my children
"No lingering death"
Sixty-four
Testing my proclamation
That I will jump
Jump from these dizzying heights
Of granite cliffs
Yes! Dash my head open
On rocks
Before landing in the icy sea
Looking now
I gulp
But of course I gulp I am ONLY 64!
Surely when I'm 74, 84, 94
I'll be brave enough
To take the dive
Now
I back away
Carefully

RED LIVES MATTER! 2014

Baby birthed from baby on the Pow! Wow!
Get 'high' way
Not the "way" it should've been
But the way it was

Girl-child of the Red People
Red Lives Matter!
But who knows or cares of your suffering?
Or your girl-child mother's suffering?
Or her mother's mother's mother's suffering?

Like shadows and ghosts flickering across
Their own lands
Barely seen
Hardly acknowledged
Flickering only for a moment
Never to REALLY shine
Just ghosts

Who gave up their lands and home?
Who forfeited their traditions and future?
Who gave up their virginity
For a bottle or a needle?
The Pow! Wow!! Get 'high' way
Is the lost highway
Too many Red ghosts drift
Along that endless road
Do Red Lives really matter?

Winter's Work 2021

Curtains of translucent rains
Veils of gusty breathes blasting
From Sky lungs
Freshening the pall of yesterday
Picking waves up to let them smash
Scouring and polishing rough stone
Chipping away at midden-shores of time
Washing-in entangled kelp tubes
With rotting deer carcass
And crab they cradle - a nest of death
Tossing purging and recycling
Churning and agitating
A winter's work is never done

AUTHOR'S NOTE

I WAS BORN on the shores of the NW Coast. My heritage is of NW Coastal Native (Tlingit and Makah) and European blood from both my mother and father. At twenty-five years old and penniless, I moved to a small island community with my two, soon to be three, children. We felt at home in this small community, Lopez island on the Salish Sea.

In my forty-three years on Lopez Island, I have lived a rich life. I'm a song keeper for our community and have helped to establish Winter and Summer Solstice traditions and Passage Rites ceremonies.

I live on a homestead without traditional plumbing, a hand pump at the sink brings us fresh spring water. No toilet, we use a composting outhouse. My husband and I eat from my large garden, drink the milk from my goats and brew cider from our orchard.

I was a doula before I'd ever heard the term. Over the course of my time here I've attended close to twenty births, most born on the island.

I am a lifelong activist for the Earth and all the natural world. I have organized protests against jet noise, whale watching, jet skis, fossil fuel, cell towers and have participated in BLM and WTO protests and kayaktivisms.

To celebrate my 40th birthday, I kayaked over 700 miles from Alaska to Lopez. Tracing the journey my ancestors took as they moved down the coast. Later, I wrote a novel interweaving my experience with the stories of my ancestors: *Paddling With Spirits: A Solo Kayak Journey.*

For this book, a big thank you to my dear friend Meredith Young for her editing help. Additional thanks for editing support to Pamela Marsten and Sorrel North

As a child I was dyslexic and could not read. I was content to observe with all my senses and create my own stories. My poems, are from my simple, treasured life.